Little Stars

# Little Stars
# SWIMMING

## A CRABTREE SEEDLINGS BOOK

Taylor Farley

CRABTREE
PUBLISHING COMPANY
WWW.CRABTREEBOOKS.COM

I love swimming.

4

I have swimming
lessons every week.

5

We **practice** blowing
bubbles in the water.

We practice kicking
our legs.

9

Some of us wear swimming **goggles**.

Some of us wear **water wings**.

12

13

I use a **kick board** to help me swim.

15

We learn different **strokes**.

16

Our **instructor** helps us and keeps us safe.

19

Swimming is lots
of fun!

# Glossary

**goggles** (GOG-uhlz): Goggles are special glasses that protect your eyes.

**instructor** (in-STRUHKT-ur): An instructor is a teacher.

**kick board** (KIK bord): A kick board is a piece of equipment that helps swimmers stay afloat.

**practice** (PRAK-tiss): Practice is doing something over and over for improvement.

**strokes** (STROKES): Strokes are movements swimmers make with their arms to move through the water.

**water wings** (WAW-tur WINGS): Water wings are full of air and are worn on the arms of someone learning to swim.

# Index

23

# School-to-Home Support for Caregivers and Teachers

Crabtree Seedlings books help children grow by letting them practice reading. Here are a few guiding questions to help the reader build his or her comprehension skills. Possible answers are included.

## Before Reading

- **What do I think this book is about?** I think this book is about swimming. It might tell us how children learn to swim.

- **What do I want to learn about this topic?** I want to learn about different ways to swim.

## During Reading

- **I wonder why...** I wonder why the children practice blowing bubbles in the water.

- **What have I learned so far?** I learned that swimmers use different tools such as goggles, water wings, and kick boards to help them swim.

## After Reading

- **What details did I learn about this topic?** I learned that swimmers learn different strokes. Strokes are arm movements.

- **Write down unfamiliar words and ask questions to help understand their meaning.** I see the word *practice* on page 6 and the word *instructor* on page 19. The other vocabulary words are listed on pages 22 and 23.

---

Library and Archives Canada Cataloguing in Publication

Title: Little stars swimming / Taylor Farley.
Other titles: Swimming
Names: Farley, Taylor, author.
Description: Series statement: Little stars | "A Crabtree seedlings book". | Includes index. |
  Previously published in electronic format by Blue Door Education in 2020.
Identifiers: Canadiana 2020037981X | ISBN 9781427129888 (hardcover) | ISBN 9780997240146 (softcover)
Subjects: LCSH: Swimming—Juvenile literature.
Classification: LCC GV837.6 .F37 2021 | DDC j797.2/1—dc23

Library of Congress Cataloging-in-Publication Data

Names: Farley, Taylor, author.
Title: Little stars swimming / Taylor Farley.
Other titles: Swimming
Description: New York : Crabtree Publishing Company, [2021] | Series: Little stars: a Crabtree seedlings book | Includes index.
Identifiers: LCCN 2020049423 | ISBN 9781427129888 (hardcover) | ISBN 9781427130068 (paperback)
Subjects: LCSH: Swimming--Juvenile literature.
Classification: LCC GV837.6 .F37 2021 | DDC 797.2/1--dc23
LC record available at https://lccn.loc.gov/2020049423

## Crabtree Publishing Company
www.crabtreebooks.com          1–800–387–7650

e-book ISBN 978-0-997240-14-6

Print book version produced jointly with Blue Door Education in 2021

Written by Taylor Farley
Production coordinator and Prepress technician: Samara Parent
Print coordinator: Katherine Berti

Printed in the U.S.A./012021/CG20201102

**Photo credits:** All images © Monkey Business Images - Shutterstock.com, except page 7 © Nic Neish - Shutterstock.com; cover and page 11 © Anton Balazh - Shutterstock.com; page 17 © Radharani - Shutterstock.com; page 21 © Studio 1One - Shutterstock.com; stars illustration on cover and throughout © Casablanka-shutterstock

**Published in Canada**
**Crabtree Publishing**
616 Welland Ave.
St. Catharines, Ontario
L2M 5V6

**Published in the United States**
**Crabtree Publishing**
347 Fifth Ave.
Suite 1402-145
New York, NY 10016

**Published in the United Kingdom**
**Crabtree Publishing**
Maritime House
Basin Road North, Hove
BN41 1WR

**Published in Australia**
**Crabtree Publishing**
Unit 3 – 5 Currumbin Court
Capalaba
QLD 4157